AFRIKA
SOLO

by

Djanet Sears

Music composed by

Allen Booth, Djanet Sears
Rudi Quammie Williams

Sister Vision
Black Women and Women of Colour Press

ISBN 0-920813-74-7

Copyright   1990 Djanet Sears

Cover and book design: Stephanie Martin
Photographs: Stephanie Martin
Photographs on pp 85, 90, 102: Peter Freund
"Afrika Solo" typeface design: Margie Bruun-Meyer
Printed and bound in Canada

Adinkra symbols on pages by Winsom
The Adinkra pattern on the pages: Nkyin Kyin means the restless wandering search, "changing one's self, playing many roles".

Canadian Cataloguing in Publication Data

Sears, Djanet
 Afrika Solo

A play
ISBN 0-920813-74-7

I. Title.

PS8587.E37A74 1990   C812'.54   C90-094300-9
PR9199.3.S43A74 1990

Published by
SISTER VISION
Black Women and Women of Colour Press
P.O. Box 217, Station E

CONTENTS

To
Winnifred, Quisbert, Rosemarie,
Terese, Celia, Kirt, Qwyn, Sharon, Donald, Donny,
Sherie, Danielle,
and Milton.

Special Thanks:

Allen Booth and Rudi Quammie Williams for their extraordinary talents, the constant encouragement, the unrelenting criticism and especially for their friendship.

Annie Szamosi for her amazing objectivity, the excellent dramaturgical skills and direction, and for agreeing to work with me on the development of this project.

Akbar Ali for his enormous assistance in helping me to gather the data included in the Afterword and Bibliography.

Maureen Fitzgerald, Kate Lushington, Ellen Pierce, Jan McIntyre, Winsom and Francois.

Acknowledgements:
Schomberg Center for Research in Black Culture, Makeda Silvera, Stephanie Martin, Peter Thurton, Barbara Brown, Sky Gilbert, Michael Miller, Theatre Fountainhead, Bell Hooks, Jackie Maxwell, Steven Bush, the Great Canadian Theatre Company, Jane Buss, Ruth Dworin, Sydne Mahone, Arcadia Housing Co-op, Lindy Papoff, Nightwood Theatre, Toronto Women's Bookstore Collective, Muriel Miguel, Rosemary Richmond, American Indian Community House, Clifton Joseph, Winston Smith, Mark Owen, Womynly Way, Esther Akinbode and the African Fashion Centre, Catherine Frazee, Monique Mojica, Raoul Rojas, Suzanne Coy, Allison Sealy-Smith, Nancy Hindmarsh, Five Minute Feminist Cabaret, Susan Feldman, Paul Thompson, Susan Cole, Ontario Black History Society, the Jamaican Canadian Association, David Wedermyer, Junior, Michael Raggett, Hartly Holder, Albert Bedward, Andre Pauzer, Canada Council, Ontario Arts Council, Secretary of State, Playwrights Union, Davida Hoyos, Carol Schwartz, Glen MacArthur, Daniel MacArthur, Jeremy MacArthur.

CHARACTERS

JANET/DJANET   A woman in her mid-twenties, British by birth, Jamaican on her Mother's side, Guyanese on her fathers, presently living in Canada, claiming Canadian citizenship.

The Janet/Djanet character also plays: V.D.; Heroine; Tarzan; Mum; Dad; Mr. Dingiswayo; Mrs. Nicolas; Tourist; Woman; Libyan;

MAN ONE   Missionary. Priest. Various character. A synthesizer player that sings and doubles on percussion as well as the accordion.

MAN TWO   Benoit's voice. David. Various characters. Man two is a percussionist that sings and plays everything from Congas to Shekere etc..

AFRIKA SOLO was first presented in Toronto by ASP in association with Factory Theatre and Theatre Fountainhead officially opening the Factory Theatre Studio Cafe on November 12, 1987 with the following cast:

JANET/DJANET/Djanet Sears
MAN ONE/ Allen Booth
MAN TWO/ Rudi Quammie Williams

Directed by Annie Szamosi; set design and costumes by Julia Tribe; lighting designed by Leslie Wilkinson; production stage managed by Alexandra Cumberland; associate produced by Terese Sears; Dramaturged by Annie Szamosi.

AFRIKA SOLO was then produced at the Great Canadian Theatre Company in Ottawa in April and May of 1989, with the following cast:

JANET/DJANET/ Djanet Sears
MAN ONE/ Allen Booth
MAN TWO/ Rudi Quammie Williams

Directed by Annie Szamosi; Set design by Roy Robitschek; Costumes designed by Esther Akinbode/Julia Tribe; Lighting designed by Phillip Cassin; Production stage managed by Laura Kennedy; Produced by ASP.

AFRIKA SOLO was also produced by Theatre Fountainhead as a tour for the High Schools in the Metropolitan Toronto Board of Education region.

'Now what effect does [the struggle over Africa]
have on us? Why should the black man in
America concern himself since he's been away
from the African continent for three or four
hundred years? Why should we concern ourselves? What impact does what happens to
them have upon us? Number one, you have to
realize that up until 1959, Africa was dominated
by the colonial powers. Having complete control
over Africa, the colonial powers of Europe pro-
jected the image of Africa negatively. They
always project Africa in a negative light: jungle
savages, cannibals, nothing civilized. Why then
naturally it was so negative that it was negative
to you and me, and you and I began to hate it.
We didn't want anybody telling us anything
about Africa, much less calling us Africans. In
hating Africa and in hating the Africans, we
ended up hating ourselves, without even realiz-
ing it. Because you can't hate the roots of a tree,
and not hate the tree. You can't hate your origin
and not end up hating yourself. You can't hate
Africa and not hate yourself.'

Malcolm X

Swing low, Sweet Chariot,
Coming for to carry me home.

Old African American spiritual

Beam me up, Scotty.

Captain James T. Kirk

THE INCANTATION

*As the lights fade to black, the sound of a
single drummer pounding out a Mandiani,
(a traditional West African rhythm), on a
Djembe (a traditional West African tenor
drum), is heard in the distance. The drum
gets louder and is soon joined by a Djundjun
(a traditional West African bass drum), a
cow bell and an assortment of other percussive sounds. The Mandiani overture
builds to a full, sensual pulse.*

Singing.

All   Mali eh cunaka, Senegale eh cunake,
                    Aah ooh nana eh dia say dah.
                    Aah, aah, aah.
                    Mali eh cunaka, Senegale eh cunake.

                    Mali eh cunaka, Senegale eh cunake,
                    Aah ooh nana eh dia say dah.
                    Aah, aah, aah.
                    Mali eh cunaka, Senegale eh cunake.

                    Mali, Senegale, Senegale, Mali,
                    Mali eh cunaka, Senegale eh cunake.

The lights slowly fade up.

THE PROLOGUE

TIME: Morning.

PLACE: Ben's room. Cotonou, Benin, West Africa.

Late morning light filters through tree shaded windows. The room contains the suggestions of traditional western furnishings, covered in striking West African decor. Ben's theme, a deep and lyrical melody, is played on a Balaphone and lightly interweaves with the Mandiani overture.

Djanet places a notepad and pen on the bed.

On the floor, in the center of the room, lie a small reinforced cardboard suitcase, a large army surplus knap sack, a Kenya bag, an ornately carved ebony walking stick and a long strip of African fabric.

Djanet places a pile of clothing and personal effects into the centre of the strip of fabric. She ties a series of knots with the two ends of the cloth, turning it into a small shoulder bag. She places the cloth bag next to the others, indicating that her packing is complete.

Djanet picks up the note pad and pen once more, and after re-reading what she has already written, she adds:

DJANET   By the time you read this letter, I will be in a
           plane somewhere over Senegal, on my way
           home. Benoit Viton Akonde, Know I love you
           muchly. Djanet.

                    *Djanet tears the letter from the note pad
                    and places it carefully on the bed. She
                    spends several moments taking in the full
                    consequence of her actions and then
                    quickly collects all of the luggage.*

                    *Suddenly, without transition, the pulsing
                    Mandiani overture is replaced by an ex-
                    plosion and the sound of human 'beat
                    boxes'. The musicians lay down a loud,
                    sensual, and heavily funky hip-hop rhythm,
                    with their mouths.*

                    Rapping.

DJANET   I took a trip to Africa to find my root,
           Let me tell ya', what I saw did not compute.

           Not everyone was starving like they tell you
           on T. V.,
           I never met an African who lived in a tree.

           They're much more concerned with wart hogs
           and vultures,
           Than for African people, their history and
           cultures.

           The kingdom of Mali was rich and strong,
           It was four months wide and four months
           long.

           Have you ever heard of Hausa land,
           Ancient Ghana, and, and, and...

Songai, Bornu, Abomey, look,
We need to rewrite the history book.

I'm gonna tell 'bout the journey and what
happened to me,
So relax and listen and you will see.

Toronto to Tombouctou,
Nairobi to Ougadougou.

Fasten your belt, takeoff 's begun,
Seven, six, five, four, three, two . . .

The music explodes.

≣≣≣≣≣≣≣≣≣≣≣≣≣

THE ACT

TIME: Same day, mid-afternoon.

PLACE: Cotonou International Airport, Benin, West Africa.

The lights flash with an explosive charge to reveal the details of an airport.

The airport is stark, clinical and modern, although there is something that quite clearly places us in Africa. To one side there is a an Air Afrique ticket booth and on the opposite side there is the suggestions of a waiting area. Mid-stage there is a tall stand to which a courtesy telephone is attached.

The rest of the stage is inhabited by a series of platforms of assorted shapes, sizes and heights. They are indicative of the specific places along the journey. Ben's room, for instance, is situated on one of these platforms.

It's early afternoon. Djanet exhaustedly drops her luggage and takes a cigarette from out of one of her bags. As she is about to light the cigarette, she notices a no smoking sign directly in front of her. She slowly returns the cigarette to it's package in her bag.

There is an urgent call for Miss Janet Sears. Mr. Benoit Akonde paging Miss Janet Sears. Would Miss Janet Sears please pick up the courtesy telephone at the Air Afrique ticket counter.

The courtesy telephone rings.

DJANET   Shit. I guess you found my note. Shit. Why
          did you have to get home so early? Shit.

          O.K., o.k., o.k., o.k., o.k., o.k. O.K.... O.K...

          The ringing stops.

          O.K., it'll take you two hours to get here at
          best, by which time I hope to be cruising at
          a steady altitude of 20.000 feet.

                *Djanet drags her luggage to the Air Afrique
                ticket counter .*

                To the ticket clerk.

          Parlez vous anglais?

                Relieved .

          Hi, I'd like to book a seat on your three
          o'clock flight... When's the next flight then?...
          Shit... Oh, O.K., standby on your three
          o'clock flight will be just fine ... Air Afrique
          flight 735... Djanet Sears... No, S. E. A. R. S...
          So how long before I can confirm a seat?...
          Twenty minutes... No; no, Great.

                *She looks around as if trying to find something
                to distract her.*

Airport   The shuttle bus to the hotel Sheraton is now
Announcer 2 boarding.

Airport   Madam Camara, ton fils Juma, t'attend par la
Announcer 3 bureau d'information central.

| Airport | Air Afrique flight 669 to Kinshasa and |
| Announcer 2 | Kisingani is now boarding at gate number 3. |

> *In the waiting area she notices that at-*
> *tached to one of the seats is a small public*
> *pay television. Dragging her luggage with*
> *her, she goes to the seat with the television,*
> *puts some coins in the appropriate slot,*
> *and turns it on.*

> *Djanet chuckles. She recognizes the pro-*
> *gram on the television. She hums the theme*
> *from Star Trek loudly.*

DJANET   L'espace, la frontiere finale. These are the
                voyages of the starship Enterprise, in French
                West Africa.

> *She sings a few bars of the theme from THE*
> *TWILIGHT ZONE.*

Do do, do do.
Do do, do do.
Do do, do do!

Oh yeh. I've seen this one... I've seen every
Star Trek ever made. Yeh, yeh, this is the one
where the entire crew of the enterprise, fall in
love.

> *She speaks directly to the audience.*

I am a T.V.. nut, no, a T.V. addict.

Name that theme?

> *She sings the theme from a popular old sci-*
> *fi t.v. series.*

Dada dada dada dada dada dadadaah,
Daaaaaaaaaaaaaah,
Da da da da da da da da da.

Dada dada dada dada dada dadadaah,
Daaaaaaaaaaaaaaaah —

O.k., let me give you another clue then.
"Danger, danger. Warning, warning. This
does not compute, this does not compute!"

You're kidding? LOST IN SPACE! The adven-
tures of the space family Robinson on their
supposed journey to Alpha Centuri. O.k.,
how about this one?

          Dada dada dada dada,
          Dat dah.
          Way too easy.
          BATMAN...

Oh, oh, oh, oh, oh! Now this is the mark of
true T.V. sci-fi-itis. 'Name that theme?'

          Ooh ooh oooh, oooh, oooh.

Oh, come on!

          Ooh ooh oooh, oooh, oooh.
          Ooh ooh ooh ooh oooh, oohh.

DR. WHO! The 900 year old time lord from
Galiffrey who travels through time and space
in a British policeman's telephone booth.
Yeh, yeh. Do you remember the Daleks? The
biological robots that look like giant laser
studded thimbles. "We are the Daleks, we
will exterminate you. Exterminate! Exterminate!".

She refers to the television.

Uh oh, Spock's in love. Look at him smile
from ear to ear. That's disgusting. Can you
blame him? She's stunning!

God, people on T.V. are just so beautiful.

And on T.V., beautiful women nearly always
have gorgeously long hair.

When I was a kid, I used to put my father's
old shirt on my head...

> *She takes her jacket off, puts it on her head
> and begins caressing her newly found
> tresses.*

And I'd toss my gorgeously long brunette
hair. Or my gorgeously long red hair. Or I'd
trim my gorgeously long blonde hair — just
so's I wouldn't get split ends.

My best friend in all the world, at the time,
had long blond hair. I was living in England
at the time. Sharon Vaughan-Davis — V.D.
for short. We go to the same school, love the
same shows on T.V. This is grounds for blood
sisterhood.

Well, V.D. comes over one weekend during
the summer holidays. And we were just
playing in the backyard — ooh, probably
barbecuing some worms or something —
when all of a sudden, there's this great big
commotion coming from my house. Someone
is screaming at the top of their lungs, "Coloured people on television! Coloured people
on television!" — Oh yeh, we were coloured

people then, we weren't black people yet. And
there were never ever any black people on
television.

*Faint strains of 'Carmen Jones' eminate
from the television. Janet becomes 8 years
old.*

JANET   Harry Belafonte and Dorothy Dandridge in
CARMEN JONES. It was so fantastic! Harry
Belafonte, so handsome and Dorothy Dandridge, so beautiful. She is the most beautiful black woman I've seen on T.V. I mean, she
looks just like Jean Harlow. Dorothy Dandridge looks exactly like Jean Harlow — 'cept
she's black!

Imitating Dorothy Dandridge .

Love's a baby that grows up wild
And he won't do what you want him to
Love is nobody's angel child
And he won't pay any mind to you

That's love...
That's love...
That's love...
That's love

*The music swells for the big finish and Janet
follows suit with much bravado — albeit,
out of key.*

To V.D.

Hey V.D.! V.D.! V.D., I'm gonna be a great
big movie star when I grow up and I'm gonna
marry Harry Belafonte. Janet Belafonte. And
we're gonna have six ki —. What's so funny?

What's so hell funny? Oh shut up, disease
face! I know it won't be so easy. I never said
it was gonna be easy — so, why don't you
just tell me something new?

In a thick cockney accent.

V.D.   Janet, I am going to devote my entire life to
plastic surgery. See, I was playing doctor
with Keith, at his house across the street.
And I was just giving him his physical this
morning and do you know that he has this
great big —

She refers to her pelvic area.

I mean, there are parts of him that definitely
need to come off — and plastic surgeons do
that.

So, one: Your bum is way too big to be a
movie star. But a plastic surgeon can cut it
off, and I'm going to be a plastic surgeon. I
haven't finished yet. Two: Your lips look like
— well, your lips are — way too thick. But I
can cut them off, I can fix them too. And
three: Your hair. Yes, your hair... Well it's
just so...

She puts her hand in Janet's hair.

...so wooly. But my Mum has that blonde
wig, yeh remember, yeh, that would look just
great!

Silence.

Janet?

Janet runs out of the room.

JANET?!

JANET   All of a sudden I don't feel so good no more. I
                 run into my mothers bedroom and I look at
                 myself in the full length mirror.

                 You know sometimes when you look into the
                 mirror and sorta' catch your own eye?

                      *She refers to the imaginary reflection
                      in front of her.*

                 I knew right then and there, that I'd grow up
                 to look exactly like Dorothy Dandridge.

                 V.D. comes in, all of a sudden being real nice
                 to me. She must have figured that I was a
                 little upset, 'cause she tells me about this
                 other show coming on t.v. that has a lot of
                 'coloured people' in it.

                      To V.D.

                 O.k., o.k., slow down, so he's the king of the
                 Jungle? No, only Doctor Doolittle can talk to
                 all the animals! And he beats up all the bad
                 guys? Wow! Lots of bad guys in Africa, eh?

                      The airport re-appears.

Airport   Mr. Benoit Akonde paging Miss Janet Sears.
Announcer   Would Miss Janet Sears please pick up the
                 courtesy telephone at the Air Afrique ticket
                 counter.

The airport announcement shatters the previous scene. Djanet tries to ignore the announcer's page and the ringing of the courtesy telephone.

DJANET   Tarzan.

Tarzan's jungle cry loudly pierces the air. The ringing stops.

Now, I didn't expect the king of the jungle to have blonde hair and blue eyes. But you soon forget about that. I mean, this guy, he really can talk to animals: Oh! Oh! Remember Cheetah the chimpanzee. Cheetah is just so intelligent — I mean Cheetah is even more intelligent than the stupid natives.

And Tarzan, he lives in this amazing tree house pad, in the middle of the jungle. It's great. It has a renovated kitchen, a bedroom with a walk in closet, and a cane floored living room with a beautiful view of the jungle skyline!

And Jane, Jane is a R.E.A.L., Total woman — I mean, wouldn't she look great in Saran Wrap?

But, like, did you ever notice, like, all the natives — I mean 'coloured people', no, black people — all the Africans, in all those Tarzan movies, are all either slaves, servants, or man-eating, savage, tribesmen. And they're always trying to... Well, let me just set you up a typical scene...

The melodramatic musical soundtrack to 'Tarzan the Apeman' is heard in the background.

These three hunters, plus a girl — there's always a girl — are on their way to find some type of rare ivory — or something. The rare elephants that have these rare ivory tusks roam freely in an area considered to be an ancient ancestral tribal burial ground. So, the Africans get wind of this group's destination and purpose, and begin practicing ancient forms of — guerilla terrorism — on the hunters. Enter Tarzan, King of the jungle.

Small fanfare.

So, they — Tarzan, the hunters and the girl — after a very tiring day in the rain forest, decide to set up camp. Lo and behold, they stumble across a very 'quaint', but luxurious six bedroom cottage cum condo — in the middle of the jungle.

Later that night, Tarzan is relaxing in his loin cloth, on the porch, enjoying the occasional jungle night breeze. In enters our heroine, (looking as gorgeously disheveled as ever).

Now, these women are truly, truly amazing. Always dressed to the nines — Coco Channel safari suit, matching safari helmet and high heeled shoes — in the middle of the jungle.

With her hand to her forehead, panting breathlessly, she says to him, she says:

In a 1940's Hollywood starlet's voice.

HEROINE   Those drums...those drums, they sound so... sooo eeevil!

DJANET   She does a considerable amount of acting at
              this point.

HEROINE   Tarzan how, how Tarzan can you bear to live
              among these... these savages?!

DJANET   And Tarzan replies, in his nice American
              accent:

                  Imitating Johnny Weissmuller.

TARZAN   This is merely a primitive method of commu-
              nication from one village to another. Get
              some sleep. You'll see, it will all be over by
              the morning.

DJANET   Next morning, drums are still going strong.
              Tarzan, the hunters and the girl, prepare to
              set off once more in search of 'IVORY IN THE
              JUNGLE', when all of a sudden, the Africans
              begin to sing. Now this to any well studied
              Tarzan fan is the cue for a tribal attack. But
              the Africans in every Tarzan movie I've seen to
              date, only know one song. It's true!

                  She sings the Tarzan tribal chant.

                  Won di
                  Won di eh my heh oh.

              I'm serious, I know it by heart!

                  Won di
                  Won di eh my heh oh.

              They don't even know another tune!

                  Won di
                  Won di eh my heh oh.

So, they start to sing the 'Won di' song.

MEN   Won di
                    Won di eh my heh oh.

                    Won di
                    Won di eh my heh oh.

                    Won di
                    Won di eh my heh oh.

DJANET   And right on cue the Africans attack —
                    "Geronimo!" —

                    Hollywood Native Indian battle cry.

MEN   Oo - Oo - Oo - Oo - Oo - Oo - Oo!!!

DJANET   No, no, no, wrong movie. Oh yeh, yeh, the
                    Africans come out of the woodwork, so to
                    speak, throwing their spears and arrows.

                    So, the hunters are caught off guard. They've
                    left their guns by the ammunition box, in a
                    clearing, 10 metres away, and can't even
                    convince one of their slaves to go and get
                    them. So the hunters are forced to rush for
                    the guns themselves, only to be cut off by a
                    single flaming arrow which soars through the
                    air towards into the ammunition box and...
                    POW!!!!!!!

                    Silence.

                    Tarzan to the rescue.

                    Big fanfare.

First he saves the heroine, from a fate worse than death — poison tipped arrow in the breast. Then he flies onto one of those conveniently placed vines, hollers and beats his chest...

Tarzan's jungle cry loudly pierces the air, once more.

And he swings bravely into the crowd of suddenly cowering tribesmen, who either die — instantaneously — or run shamelessly to their grass huts down the road.

The lights become very intimate as Djanet flashes back to a conversation with Ben.

Ben? Did you see Tarzan movies in Benin when you where growing up? Did you know that Cheetah the Chimpanzee had such a crush on Johnny Weissmuller that the make-up artist had to paint Cheetah's erection black so it wouldn't be seen on camera. It's true!

The moment instantly dissolves.

It was lunch time and we were all lined up in the school cafeteria, V.D., Keith and I, awaiting today's gourmet pickings.

Janet picks up an imaginary food tray.

JANET   The roast beef looks wounded. Mash potatoes—from the powder, and cooked cauliflower.

Now, every time I see cooked cauliflower I get an overwhelming urge to vomit. And as they

                    slopped the cooked cauliflower on to my plate
                    I was trying to figure out a way to convince
                    Keith to eat it. Keith would eat anything.
                    Keith even ate the worms we barbecued in my
                    back yard. And even Keith didn't want 'em.
                    Then, V.D. says she knows a good way of
                    picking which one of the three of us is gonna
                    have to eat my cooked cauliflower and she
                    starts in with...

V.D.   Enie, meanie, minie, mo, catch a nigger by
                    the —

JANET   Hey, V.D.! Don't say nig — the 'N' word! My
                    mum said, you're not supposed to say that
                    word. She said, it's the nastiest word you can
                    say to any black person...   V.D. don't ... V.D.
                    I'm seri..! V.D.!!

                    But she just kept saying it, over and over and
                    over again.

V.D.   Nigger, nigger, nigger, nigger, nigger, nigger,
                    nigger, nigger, nigger.

Janet   V.D! V.D., I'm not... I'm not...

V.D.   Nigger, nigger, nigger, nigger —

JANET   V.D.! V.D.! V.D.!

V.D.   Nigger, nigger, nigger, nigger, nigger, nig—

JANET   And I slap her. I slap her.

                    And she falls right back. And, she just
                    stares up at me, like she doesn't know who I
                    am. And this bright red mark the shape of
                    my hand appears on her face. Then all of a

sudden she gets up and runs to the back of
the cafeteria.

Now sitting right at the back of the cafeteria is
Terminal. Terminal is V.D.'s big brother.
V.D.'s big brother is so big, he's the only kid
in our entire school who doesn't wear a
school uniform because they don't come that
large. I mean, he's the kind of kid that at 11
years old, goes around scalping Barbie dolls,
just for fun.

So down the aisle comes Terminal V.D., and
V.D., right behind him with my red hand
mark on her face.

To Terminal.

Terminal, she called me nig— the 'N' word!
My mum told us not to say that word. My
mum said the 'N' word is the baddest —

Silence.

JANET   And I don't remember anything after that.

Try and imagine what it would feel like if
someone took a Mack truck and rammed it
into your face. Everyone thought I was dead.
But oh no, I recover only to survive seven
whole months of:

       All I want for Christmas is my two
       front teeth, My two front teeth...

Terminal and V.D. were transferred to another
school. But I saw her once more after that.
She was on my street — must have been
going to Keith's house — and I was pretend-

ing not to see her. And she stopped, turned right to me, on the other side of the street, and screamed out:

V.D.   Why don't you just go back to where you come from!

JANET   And you know I would have marched right across that street and slapped her again, only I couldn't exactly figure out what she was talking about. I really had no idea what she meant...

JANET   Well, my mum's from Jamaica.

                Reggae music floats above her.

                Singing.

MAN ONE   Jammin'. We're jammin'.
MAN TWO   We're jammin'.
MAN ONE   We're jammin'.

JANET   But my dad, he's from Guyana.

                A popular calypso intertwines itself with the reggae music.

                Singing.

MAN TWO   Jean and Dinah, Rosetta and Clementina.

JANET   And I was born in England, the same as V.D.

                Singing.

                    God save our gracious queen,
                    Long live our noble queen,
                    God save our queen.

All three musics are heard simultaneously.

WHERE THE HELL AM I FROM?!!

DJANET   Years later, by which time I'm the proud
              owner of four passports, seriously, I have a
              Canadian passport, a British passport, a
              Guyanese passport and a Jamaican passport,
              I again think of V.D . Where the hell am I
              from?

                    *Djanet picks up her luggage once again
                    and drags it over to the Air Afrique ticket
                    counter.*

                    To the ticket clerk.

DJANET   Hi... I'm on standby... Can you check...
              Djanet Sears, yes... Great! One-way please.
              Smoking... O.k., non-smoking... Great!
              Just this. The rest I'll take on as hand lug-
              gage... Thank you... Ah, passports? Take
              your pick, I've got four.

                    *Djanet throws four passports on to the
                    counter.*

                    Rapping.

                    If I was born in Gadansk am I a pole,
                    I maybe solidarnosc, but I've got soul.

                    I talk like a Brit from Saskatoon,
                    And let me tell ya, it's no damn
                    honeymoon.

                    I call one day about a room for rent,
                    When I get to the house, he says "It
                    just went".

And it happens all the time and it
makes me wanna foam.
I just gotta get away, I'm gonna find
my home.

*Djanet clicks her heels together (a la Wizard
of Oz).*

There's no place like home. There's no
place like home. There's no place like
home.

My mum and Dad saw me off at Buffalo
Airport.

*The family theme, a slow and disjointed
reggae and calypso fusion, can be heard.*

JANET   This was it. Here I was going back to mother
Africa. I would be retracing the steps of my
ancestors, my ancestors, after 400 years.

My flight was cancelled. MY FLIGHT was
CANCELLED — until the next morning.

I've never seen fog that bad. Me, my mum
and my dad book into a hotel across the
street.

And my mum was saying to me, how much of
a coincidence it is that I should be leaving
home to go abroad on my own — she was
exactly my age when she first left Jamaica to
travel to England to study. She even tells me
about her first part-time job, scrubbing the
cold stone floors of the Tower of London. She
nearly died of Pneumonia — they treated her
so badly there.

In a Jamaican accent.

MOM   If you ever get fed up of traveling, or you just
               want to come home, don't think twice about
               calling.

                    *The lights change as Djanet flashes back to
                    Ben.*

DJANET   You know Ben, I've never been to the Tower of
               London. I lived in London for fifteen years
               and my mum would always refuse to take me
               there.

                    The moment dissolves.

JANET   And my father - my father is the kind of man
               who only says important things. You know
               like:

                    In a Guyanese accent.

DAD   Get your career together before you even
               think of getting married.

JANET   Or...

DAD   Education. Child, you are nowhere without
               education.

JANET   And I guess he figured that he shouldn't send
               me off into the big wide world without some
               important lesson. Some anecdote that he
               could give me that would help me through the
               bad times and support me through the good
               times. And you know what he told me? He
               said...

DAD   Never forget to wash your underwear!

JANET   And you know, I'm still trying to decipher the
true meaning, the true profundity in that
statement.

At the departure gate the next morning, as I
waved good-bye, I tried to impress their image
onto my mind. So I'd never forget.

To her parents.

Don't forget to write. Come and visit me
when I settle down!

Bye!

Janet climbs the stairway onto the ferry.

Tunisia. Tunisia.

'A Night in Tunisia' can be heard.

All I could think about was that Dizzie
Gellespie song and kissing the African soil.
Yeh, that would be my own ceremony of
return. Yeh, the first thing that I'll do is to
kiss the African soil.

The sea was rough that day and the ferry was
3 hours late. Suddenly I see the shores of
Africa. The soft rolling mountains of Tunisia.
The tip of the continent I would never leave.

*'A Night in Tunisia' crossfades into the sound
of turbulent Mediterranean Sea waves.*

This is it! This is it!! The waves are so high,
though. I'm not even really supposed to be
up on deck. The bathrooms are full of people
— throwing up. Can you imagine, here it is,
my first impression of glorious Africa—

She pukes.

*Janet quickly recovers and takes a first step
onto the African continent.*

Tunisia. It wasn't just any dock. It was an
African dock. Three hours late, but here at
last, here at last. Thank God almighty, I'm
here at last.

Rapping.

The Passport was stamped and the visa was
checked, But there was one more permit I had
to get.

When the immigration officer started to say

MAN TWO   The transportation office will open Monday.

JANET   I looked to the left and I looked to the right,
               What the hell you saying, it's Thursday night,
               now.

               Look, I want to speak to the supervisor
               Mister?

MAN TWO   What you see is what you get, I am the super-
               visor, sister!

MAN TWO   Friday is a holy day, on the weekends they
               close, That leaves Monday morning, bright
               and early, six on the nose.

JANET   I was so pissed off, I was sure I would boil.
               And, you'll never catch me dead kissing
               Tunisian soil!!

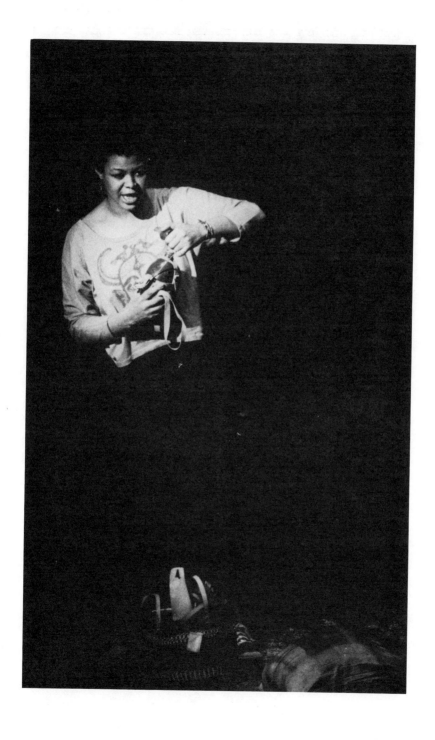

*The earth under her feet visibly changes.
Janet finds herself walking on sand.*

The desert is like nowhere else in the world.
It drew me into its womb like a lost child.
Here a few basic designs of sand, gravel and
mountains are used repeatedly and stretched
to their limits, like a trial run in landscape
architecture gone wrong.

Living in the Sahara is like living on another
planet. Yeh, I felt as if I were on Mars.

*Janet takes a mirror compact from out of
her bag and uses it as a Star Trek commu-
nicating device. As she opens the compact we hear the Star Trek communicator
beep.*

Captain's log: Star date: One nine eight four
point two two five: The terrain is unfamiliar,
oceanic in scale, flat and unchanging for days
of travel. It's amazing. 360 degrees of pure
sand and sky.

*The communicator beeps as she closes
and replaces the compact. She takes out
a small water cannister.*

It's weird how you get used to having sand
everywhere, all the time. In your hair, in your
clothes, in your sleeping bag, in your mouth,
up your nose, in your air tight flinking camera lens. But one thing you never get used to
is desert water. I became a self-proclaimed
water gourmet.

There was this one water I filled up with in
Timiouahne. So this water, O.k.? It's grey.
I'm serious. The more I drink of this water,
the thirstier I get. It has the consistency of
liquefied Jello and tastes like Maalox. I even
tried mixing it with Tang or Lemonade. Can
you imagine lemon flavoured Pepto Bismal?

In the driest parts of the Sahara, I was limited
to 2 litres of water a day. To drink and bathe
in. I got it down to an art. I can wash my
entire body in one cup of water.

*Janet pours water from the cannister into a
small bowl.*

But on those days when I did fill up with
water, luxury. I would fill a small wash basin
practically to its brim and find a secluded
spot behind some nearby sand dune. The
sun would have just left the sky and the
moon would have already taken it's place. I'd
take off all my clothes — feel the warm air
against my skin. The stars flickering in the
immense sky. And I'd slowly wash.

It was a ritual, I guess.

She performs a washing ritual.

I'd wash the sand from out of my eyes, from
out of my ears, from off my skin. I'd wash the
sand from out of my mouth and from between my toes. But I'd never be able to wash
the African sand from out of my soul.

Singing.

> Twinkle, twinkle, little star,
> How I wonder what you are.
> Up above the world so high,
> Like a diamond in the sky.
> Though I know not what you are,
> Twinkle, twinkle, little...
>
> Stars like diamonds,
> Alone under the crowded sky,
> Makes you wonder why.
> What is in this human heart,
> That longs for love and that reaches for
> the...
>
> Stars like diamonds.
> I long for someone to hold me tight,
> And share this wondrous sight.
> Arms wide open, let me in.
> Then I'll out shine these bright pulsating...
>
> Stars like diamonds.
> Isolated, far from home,
> How much longer will I roam.
> I seek a place where I fit in,
> And I'll search until I find it,
> I'll look up around and behind it,
> I'll know it when I get there,
> 'cause I'll sleep within your arms under the
> stars.

One day, after weeks of sand or gravel plains,
on the horizon appeared one of the most
beautiful oasis' I ever saw. Like in a mirage,
a mountain of green appeared from out of
nowhere.

The oasis town of Djanet. D. J. A. N. E. T. It means paradise in Arabic. The water in Djanet gushed out of the earth, out of her core, clear and abundantly. It tasted so sweet.

Djanet is also the gateway to the secrets of the Tassili plateau. The ten thousand year old Saharan rock paintings. Two of the more famous paintings depict beings that wear helmets over their heads and space suits. In one of the paintings, the one called the Martian, the being has only one eye. In fact experts have actually speculated on visitations from outer space.

Have you noticed that if an anthropologist goes out and studies an ancient 'third world' culture, and he finds knowledge or traditions way in advance of his own, he always ends up speculating on visitations from outer space. I've noticed that.

Anyhow, to be able to see these rock paintings, one has to get written permission from the chief tourist officer in Djanet. You see, the department does not allow unphysically fit or overweight visitors to climb the four thousand meter volcanic mountain route to the paintings. (It seems that past experiences with unfit visitors have resulted in emergency rescues by helicopter for cases of heart attack and physical exhaustion).

But I line up outside Mr. Dingiswayo's office door anyhow.

She walks to the end of an imaginary queue.

Oh shit! He's asking that woman in front of me to stand aside, and she's not even that fat. Shit, he's never going to let me go now.

Confidence, Janet. Confidence!

I hand him my form and he looks up at me. (Probably assessing the bulk.)

In a deep North African accent.

DINGISWAYO Where do you come from?

JANET   Canada, sir.

DINGISWAYO Oh Canada, eh?

JANET   (He's probably never seen a black North American woman in his life.)

               But my ancestors are from Africa. We've been away for over 400 years!

DINGISWAYO Ah, like Kunta Kinte, eh?   Here, enjoy your journey!

JANET   The four hour climb nearly killed me. But I made it.

               Janet takes out a camera and begins to take photographs.

The paintings are spectacular. Fifty or sixty major works. They range from ochre and charcoal impressions of elephants, antelope, lions, wild animals, to detailed etchings of people with herds and herds of cattle — in the

middle of the desert. I had to keep looking around, just to remind myself of where I was. And these were African people.

You see, over 4500 years ago when the green Sahara began turning to sand, these people migrated. Some southward where they developed a Kingdom called Great Zimbabwe which stretched from the Zambezi to the Mpopo rivers. And some to the north-east, to Nubia and Egypt, where they developed one of the greatest and most powerful civilizations in antiquity.

The lights become drastically brighter.

Then all of a sudden. There I am, in Mrs. Nicholas' class — there I am, 7 years old, the only black kid in my class.

In a high pitched upper class British accent.

NICHOLAS   I am disgusted at the way those coloured people are reacting to the death of Martin Luther King. They are rioting in the streets, Looting innocent merchants, even killing people. We did not rampage nor kill people when John F. Kennedy died, did we? I am not surprised that the American police are locking them up behind bars. Civilized human beings do not act that way.

JANET   And she's looking right at me. Mrs. Nicholas. And I don't know what to say. All I can think is —

Her hand up shoots into the air.

Miss, I have to pee.

Djanet flashes back to Ben.

DJANET   Civilized human beings, eh? What is it you
              said Ben? 'Civilization is merely the art of
              building cities.'

              The moment dissolves.

              *'Ba ba black sheep' and 'Mary had a little
              lamb' are heard being played very simply
              in the background.*

Once upon a time, a European traveller, while
in southern most Africa doing some geological
research, (as well as some missionary work
on the side), became very good friends with
some Zulu people. One day, one of the Zulu
men told the European of an amazing site,
and he and a few of his Zulu friends took the
European traveller to see this awe inspiring
vision.

When they arrived the European was breath-
taken.
"What is it called?", the European cried.
"Called?", replied the Zulu. "It is called 'the
great water fall'."
"The great water fall, eh," repeated the European.

So right then and there the European re-
named and christened the great wonder
himself. He christened it Victoria, after his
great Queen. And from that day forward, generation after generation have read in the great
history books: Victoria Falls, discovered by --
David Livingston.

              The nursery rhymes stops abruptly.

You know, nothing exists until a white man
finds it!

Djanet flashes back to Ben.

Remember the french map in the palace,
Ben. It gave away the Frenchman's true first
impressions of Benin and it's people. They
called the country , 'Le Royoume de Judas',
'The Kingdom of Judas'.

The moment dissolves.

*Back in the airport, Djanet takes a note
pad and pen out of one of her bags and
begins to write.*

JANET   Dear Ben... I know that you —

*She rips the paper out, throws it away and
begins   to write again .*

Dear Ben... Je sais que — je sais que —

*She rips this one out too and begins once
more.*

Dear Ben - -

*This time she crosses his name out replaces
it with:*

JANET   Dear Mum and Dad...

*Janet is immediately transported back to
the Sahara. She continues writing.*

The rock paintings in Djanet are ten thousand year old. That's four hundred genera-
tions ago. Three hundred and ninety-eight
point two grandmothers ago. Can you imagine, people lived ten thousand years ago in
Djanet? Love Janet.
*She crosses out her signature and replaces
it with:*

D. J. A. N. E. T.

Rapping.

DJANET   What if Jomo Kenyatta was a Robert
                        or Paul,
                        And Miriam Makeba was known as
                        Lucille Ball.

                        You see there's pride in a name and I
                        can see
                        Why Cassius changed his name to
                        Muhammed Ali.

                        A rose by any other name would smell
                        as sweet,
                        But an African called Sears sounds so
                        offbeat.

                        Though my family's Sears, you know
                        what's more?
                        We're related to some Sears with a de-
                        partment store.

                        Though Janet rhymes with planet,
                        what's in a name?
                        I'll add a 'D' to the beginning and it's
                        Djanet again.

Djanet with a 'D' not Janet with a 'J',
Djanet with a 'D' not Janet with a 'J',

I changed my being and spirit this
way!!

Airport   Mr. Benoit Akonde paging Miss Janet Sears.
Announcer   Would Miss Janet Sears please pick up the
              courtesy telephone at the Air Afrique ticket
              counter.

              *Djanet shouts as if trying to kill the incessant
              ringing of the courtesy telephone.*

DJANET   HOT!

              The ringing stops.

              It was so hot. Nearly 120 degrees Fahrenheit
              in the shade. It was so hot here all I could
              think about was how cold it was that first
              winter in Canada.

              What a culture shock — London, England to
              Saskatoon, Saskatchewan. I was fifteen, the
              height of my pubertal social life, and the only
              black kid in my entire school, now. The other
              kids would even come up to me and ask to
              touch my hair and stuff.

              And look, I was used to the cold. London,
              England isn't exactly the Montego Bay of
              Europe, you know. But this was ridiculous. I
              nearly freaked right flinking out the first time
              the hairs in my nose froze. And snow...

Singing in a broad calypso style.

Saskaberia, Saskatchewan,
The true north flinking pole.
Frost biting ya fingers,
Chill eating ya skin,
Snow up in ya asshole,
The air so cold it sting.
The Earth was made to live on
I know I read it in a book,
But I just can't go on living
Like a palm tree in a toque.

Now everybody sing...

And here I was only days away from Tombouctou, where in 1324, one of the worlds
first universities was built. Here I was only
days away from Tombouctou, thinking about
snow. Dreaming about a nice cool, freezing
cold Blue, or Molson Golden. And thank
God I'm in Mali now, because you can't get
beer in Algeria.

See, Algeria is a muslim country. You know,
the women are covered from head to toe in
black — from head to toe — in the middle of
the desert.

O.k., I've got a good one for you. If Buck-
wheat became a Muslim, what would he be
called?

Kareem Of Wheat!   O.k... O.k... O.k...

Djanet flashes back to Ben.

I couldn't believe my ears. Here we were in
the fetish market, in the voodom section, and
I ask you about the different Yoruba Gods
and what they stood for and you say:
"I don't know. I don't know, I'm Catholic."
Catholic!

The moment dissolves.

Catholic. Even my short lived excursion into
Christianity taught me that had I not been
lucky enough to be the descendant of a slave,
I would be among the millions of heathenistic
savages, basically doomed for hell barring a
visit from one of the missionaries they were
sending down to the 'dark continent' to save
us sinners from an eternity of darkness. Oh
Ben!

MISSIONARY   We come as members of a superior race to
spiritually elevate the more degraded parts of
humanity.

Singing.

ALL   Onward Christian soldiers
Into heathen lands.
Prayer book in your pockets,
Rifles in your hands.
Take the happy tidings
Where trade can be done,
Spread the peaceful gospel
With the Gatling gun.

*Rock Of Ages is sung in Swahilli and can be
heard in the background.*

Djanet puts her hammock together.

≣ ≣ ≣ ≣ ≣ ≣ ≣ ≣ ≣ ≣ ≣ ≣ ≣

DJANET   Just like Kenya. I mean, I was in Kenya,
              living with the Turkana — you know, the
              people who stretch their necks with layers
              upon layers of glass beads?

              Well, I'd just hitched my tent to the back of
              Mr. David Malequa's grass hut. David and I
              got along real well. See, I was almost fluent
              in swahilli by now and David Malequa knew
              almost 17 words in English.

              This may just be it. This may just be what I've
              been looking for.

              Now this teeny tiny village of about, oh, some
              70 people, or so, seemed to be able to support
              two fully constructed brick churches. One's
              Baptist and the other one's Catholic.

              One afternoon, David Malequa, my Turkana
              host, tells me that a priest from the land
              where the big Catholic chief lives, is coming
              here to Turkana, to give mass.

              When I get to the church, aside from finding
              the entire village there — it seems that the
              entire village plays the role of congregation for
              both churches — I also notice, that all the
              women are wearing rosary beads at the
              bottom of their already impressive collection
              of glass beads. This is my first clue to why
              Catholicism is still thriving in Turkana land!

              Now the visiting priest isn't from Rome at all,
              this guy's from Barcelona. But, you see, I
              don't realize until 5 minutes into the Mass,
              that it's actually English he's speaking. And,
              listen to this, David, the guy who's hut I'm

hitching my tent to, is standing next to the
priest, translating the priest's English into
swahilli. Please recall that David only knows
17 words in English. And even I can't understand what the priest is saying.

Oh yeah, I forgot one thing. David is Muslim.

The Swahilli hymn stops abruptly.

PRIEST   Hallelujah!

                David translates the English into Swahilli.

DAVID   Yesu ni M'luya!

                *Djanet translates David's interpretation back
                into English.*

DJANET   Jesus was a member of the Luya tribe.

PRIEST   Jesus Christ was a Jew!

DAVID   Hata Yesu alitumia choo!

DJANET   Even Jesus went to the toilet.

                Holy... Leave North America, and come to live
                in a teeny tiny village with two churches?

                She quickly dismantles the hammock.

                When I was younger, all this darkness was
                being heaped upon me. "It will be a 'black
                day' when the lord descends to judge us all
                if every man woman and child has not heard
                the word of Jesus Christ our saviour." Black
                day, eh? Well, if it's going to be a black day, I
                suspect that I will do very well!

Back in the airport, Djanet pulls out a cross-word puzzle.

O.k.. Nine letters that mean, 'a longing for familiar circumstances that are now remote'? My love life. Doesn't fit any way. Oh, oh, nostalgic. Now, seven letters that mean, 'ancestor worshipper', beginning with 'C'? Cannibal? Eating someone could be a form of worship. Maybe not. Ancestor worshipper, beginning witn 'C'?

No, no, no, no, no. Not nostalgic, nostalgia. So seven letters that mean 'ancestor worshipper', beginning with the letter 'A', is animist.

Dogon drumming begins.
The Dogons are Animists. They worship nature and the spirits of their ancestors. The neat thing about worshipping your ancestors is that you live your life knowing you too will become an ancestor one day. Sure, I could learn to get into that.

Putting away her crossword puzzle she makes her way towards what becomes the Dogon village.

The Dogons live in areas that are difficult to access. That's why neither the Muslims nor the Christians have managed to convert them from their 'savage ways'.

As you look down on to the Dogon village from the mountain top, you can see a collection of houses and granaries all crowded together, flat roofs of clay alternating with cone-shaped roofs of straw.

Some of the Dogons would point or stare, others would actually come up to me and say something that sounded like "Dogoni, Dogoni?" As if to say, you're one of us, aren't you? You're one of us.

But even with a translator there, I felt an enormous communication gap between myself and these people. These people I wanted to know.

I decided that I should be moving on. I had picked up a few words in Dogon by now. I woke up early that morning and I made my way along the narrow streets of light and shade, to a large rock in a open area. This I figured could be considered somewhat the centre of town. I sat down on this rock which divided two pathways and proceeded to say hello in Dogon to every man, woman or child that passed me by. I stopped everyone.

Ouh sayawa?

MAN ONE   Ouh man a sayawa.

DJANET   Sayawa?

MAN ONE   Sayawa.

MAN TWO   Ouh sayawa?

DJANET   Ouh man a sayawa.

MAN TWO   Sayawa?

DJANET   Sayawa.

It felt so good, just saying 'hello, how are you?' Sayawa? Sayawa — Geez, I wonder if that's where, 'say what?', comes from?

Airport Announcer Mr. Benoit Akonde paging Miss Janet Sears. Would Miss Janet Sears please pick up the courtesy telephone at the Air Afrique ticket counter.

The courtesy telephone rings.

Djanet takes a knife and a large ripe mango from out of her bag. She cuts the fruit open and eats it succulently as West African 'high life' music surrounds her.

DJANET In most of rural Africa, the market place is the centre of the world. Like Wall St. A barrage of sound, colour, smells and things I'd never seen before. Like the Eaton Centre* the Saturday before Christmas.

I must have hit every market place from Tombouctou to Nairobi. It's the only real place you can actually just sit and people watch. And the people: Most of the men in West Africa wear long regal gowns and tall embroidered hats. And the women... Aah, the women.

I began to notice that a lot of the women, well — had behinds that were just like mi — very well developed. Yeh, they had these voluptuously developed hips. And their lips, their

---

*   The name, Eaton Centre, can be substituted for the name of the most popular shopping centre in the region.

lips were sensuous and full. And their hair —
oh, you should have seen some of the coiffs
and the many intricate styles of head wraps.
God, this is beautiful! The women adorn
themselves with these stunning fabrics and
jewelry.

> *She puts the mango down and picks up*
> *one of the lengths of West African fabric*
> *that adorn the stage.*

Isn't this just gorgeous! I bought seventeen of
these in one marketplace.

> *The West African 'high life' crossfades into*
> *a Masai rhythm. Djanet slowly wraps the*
> *material around her body , folding and*
> *pleating the material into a traditional*
> *West African style.*

I lived with the Masai for three months.
They're amazing people. They're basically a
nomadic people who take care of their many
herds of cattle. You know, the more cattle
you have, the more status you acquire. Well,
their concept of beauty is completely different. The men and women wrap themselves in
layers and layers of loose material. The
women wear pounds of beautifully beaded
jewelry.   In fact, the women stretch their ear
lobes and the closer her ear lobe is to her
shoulder the more beautiful she is.

Like I mean, Dorothy Dandridge would not
have made it here.

I spoke fluent Swahilli at the time as well as a
few words in Maa, the Masai language, and I
had the privilege of playing tour guide from

time to time, for the tourists who came down to the Masai's 'encang', their small encampment. And the questions some tourists would ask. One woman, after taking a tour of the Masai village, actually had the gall to say...

In a broad white southern U.S. accent.

TOURIST   Is the Masai's lack of conventional clothing in any way linked to some type of native sexual rite?

DJANET   On the other hand, after the tourists had left, the Masai would hold major dialectic discussions on why Westerners wear clothes that hold in their farts!

                Wearing the West African wrap in some way transforms her. The metamorphosis begins. 'That's love', the song from 'Carmen Jones' is reprieved with subtle West African rhythmic adjustments.

                That's love,
                That's love,
                That's love,
                That's love.

It was really quite eerie, you know. In some parts of Togo and Benin, on the West African coast, I began to see familiar faces. I began to recognize people. There was this one man, selling souvenirs, at the grand market in Lome, that was the spitting image of my uncle Jim. I must of used up about two roles of film just taking pictures of him to show my Dad.

                Pointing to some passers by.

Auntie Norma!

Oh my God, uncle Vibert.

Ratid hole, there's Mr. Ackee, the man who owns the Jamaican Patty shop up on Eglinton*.

And by the way, Eddie Murphy's double's name is Senou Batande, and he lives at 79 Magamate St., Ouida, The Republic of Benin. I'm serious!
At the Grand Marche, the grand marketplace here in Cotonou, the capital of Benin, a woman selling mangoes, passion fruit, bananas and an assortment of birth control pills asked me if I was an 'American noire', a black American. So I explain to her that I live in Canada. Then she said something that surprised me.

In a broad west African accent.

WOMAN   So you did come back.

DJANET   Pardon me?

WOMAN   They always said that you would return. The legends say that those who where taken away by the European on their big ships would return one day.

Silence.

At that moment I knew I'd arrived.   Here at

---

*   'On Eglinton', can be substituted for any well known area, or street name, populated by Caribbean people or Caribbean stores: i.e. 'in Brooklyn'.

last was the gold carpet laid out to greet me. It all felt so familiar, yet, at the same time, so unfamiliar. I mean, I was home, but I didn't know anyone or anything here. Somewhere in the last four hundred years I'd lost a major connection with this place.

I should have stayed in Benin right then and there, but I'd booked my passage to Nigeria already — I had my bus ticket in my pocket.

I wanted to leave her some memento of my passing. I had a CITY-TV T-shirt and a pin of the Canadian flag — the T-shirt was dirty, so I gave her the pin. I'll never forget her.

The airport re-appears.

Airport
Announcer

Mr. Benoit Akonde paging Miss Janet Sears. Would Miss Janet Sears please pick up the courtesy telephone at the Air Afrique ticket counter.

The courtesy telephone rings. This time Djanet approaches it.

DJANET

Oh Ben.

The ringing stops.

One day I came across a book in the library. I'm a procrastinator. I had an essay due the next day on teenage skin problems for my health class, and I was looking in the index for a book on black heads and acne. There was nothing under black heads, but I came across this one book called, 'Black people,

black kingdoms'. I immediately vetoed check-
ing dermatitis under the subject listings and
jotted down the call number for this 'black
kingdoms' book.

This book was the first truly amazing book I'd
ever read — not counting 'The Jackson Five
Story'. I read about the many West African
Kingdoms, their kings and queens, princes
and princesses. Nzingha the renowned
warrior queen in the kindom of Ngola. Mansa
Musa, emperor of the great Kindom of Mali.
Yaa Asantewa, queen mother of the Ashanti
state of Ejisu.

It had glorious pictures of palaces and struc-
tures of worship. I never learned any of this in
school. There was even a chapter that stated
that there is scientific basis for the ancient
potions of African witch-doctors, that western
medicine has only begun to investigate.

I began this fantasy about being a long lost
African princess. I could be royalty and not
even know it.

Djanet flashes back to Ben.

Benoit Viton Akonde, when you told me that
your great grandfather was the last king of
Abomey, I nearly croaked. (My sisters will die
when they hear this one.)

The moment dissolves.

So, I'm on my way to Lagos, when...

Rapping.

At the border to Nigeria
A scene of mass hysteria

Hoards of people can't get through
No-one knows just what to do.

Excuse me sir, open up the gate,
I must be in Lagos at eight.

MAN TWO   Turn around, please you must go back
                 Or I'll start acting like a maniac

MAN TWO   This border is shut for several days
                 Unforeseen technical delays.

DJANET   Look I don't want to misconstrue
                 So I ask them to tell me why can't I get
                 through.

MAN ONE   Our currency is devaluating
                 Contraband, blackmaket is escalating.

MAN TWO   Psychic quasi rent, fiscal
                 reconciliation
                 Zero base market force needs
                 rectification.

DJANET   I didn't understand what he was
                 saying to me
                 You see I failed economics at
                 university.

                 Hey, the poetry's nice sir, but what are
                 you saying
                 Am I going to Nigeria or am I staying?

MAN TWO   The borders are closed to change the
                 colour of our money,
                 Our currency's the Nira - honey.

DJANET	The plates are now in England to be printed — I learn.
MAN ONE	The borders are closed 'till they return.
DJANET	Six days later things get weird.
BOTH MEN	Two barrels of new Nira have disappeared!
DJANET	Two barrels of new Nira have disappeared!

She sings a few bars of the theme from TWILIGHT ZONE.

Do do, do do.
Do do, do do.
Do do, do do!

So, I'm stuck in Benin. And amongst other things, I've contracted a severe case of the 'I am sick of living in a tent' blues. I mean, here I was camped out behind the kitchen of a two star hotel. But it was conveniently right across the street from the Benin Sheraton Hotel - which had a grand five star rating.

One of the interesting things about the Benin Sheraton was that once inside, I may as well have been sitting in the Four Seasons — you know, at Avenue Road in Yorkville* . It was plush. Filled with plush carpets, plush furniture, even the food was plush.

---

*   The name and location of this hotel can be substituted with the name a location of the most exclusive hotel in the region.

The stand to which the courtesy telephone is attached revolves to reveal a bar. Piano lounge music can be heard in the background.

So, here I am standing at the bar drinking my Grand Marnier and orange juice — listen, I have slept in a tent every night for the last seven months, the least I can do is treat myself.

She drinks.

Then the waiter tells me that a certain gentleman would like to buy me another round. Well, I have only seen this kind of thing happen in the movies.

The waiter points to the gentleman in question.

She glances in his direction.

Oh my God, he's a knock out. Tall, dark, very dark and very handsome. Our eyes meet across the crowded room.

After about an hour, or so, of exchanged glances, I find myself in complete lust with this man. Oh... Oh no — he's leaving. Oh... Oh God — no — he's coming this way. Oh. He's coming over to the bar. Oh my Go...

Djanet smiles widely.

Hello! Oh, of course, please join me. (He's a Libyan expatriate. He's even more beautiful up close. What slender hands. What a charming smile. What a — oh shut up Djanet, you're beginning to sound carnivorous.)

≘ ≘ ≘ ≘ ≘ ≘ ≘ ≘ ≘ ≘ ≘ ≘ ≘ ≘

In a lush, sexy Libyan accent.

LIBYAN   You are on your way to Nigeria, are you not?"

DJANET   (Oh God, he's psychic too!) Yes, but the
                borders are closed, they say —

LIBYAN   I know, I saw you at the border last week. I
                am also stranded...

DJANET   (What luck, he's stranded too.)

LIBYAN   I was wondering, would you be interested —
                in buying some freshly printed Nigerian Nira?

                Pause.

DJANET   You mean... The stuff that they've just had
                printed in England?

                The Libyan smiles widely.

LIBYAN   Hmm hhmn.

DJANET   You mean... The stuff that they haven't even
                distributed yet?

LIBYAN   Hmm hhmn.

DJANET   At which point a beautiful black lady, with
                long flowing braids, taps him on the shoulder
                and whispers in his ear. He smiles. He then
                tells me that he has to leave and sights
                important business.

LIBYAN   But here is my room and telephone number,
                should you need my assistance.

DJANET   They leave the bar, arm in arm.

                What an asshole. Why do I always fall for
                assholes. I swear he will be the last one.

                The bar disappears.

                *Djanet mutters an array of sorrys and
                excuse mes as she attempts to get to an
                empty seat in the middle of an imaginary
                row of already seated people.*

                So imagine. Here I am in Benin, a tiny little
                country in West Africa, at an outdoor cinema,
                watching:

                She sits.

                Maurice Chevalier, Leslie Carron and Louis
                Jordan in 'GIGI'.

                *In a Maurice Chevalier's singing voice, while
                accompanying himself on a French accor-
                dion.*

MAN ONE   Thank heaven for liddle (sic) girls...

DJANET   This is weird, this is really weird!

                So it starts to pour and everyone rushes to
                the lobby, but me — look, I've always wanted
                to see the end of GIGI.

                Then I hear this voice:

MAN ONE   Thank heaven for liddle girls...

                In a deep French/West African accent.

MAN TWO   It's nice and dry under here.

DJANET	(Oh no, another black-market-Romeo.) No thank you very much, that's very kind of you.
MAN ONE	Thank heaven for liddle girls...
MAN TWO	Are you with the peace corps?
DJANET	No, I'm afraid not.
MAN ONE	Thank heaven for liddle girls...
MAN TWO	You must be with CUSO then?
DJANET	(I knew it, I knew it. I can now spot an asshole within 30 metres of me.) No I'm not with CUSO. I'm just a traveller.
MAN TWO	Ah uh!
MAN ONE	Thank heaven for liddle girls...
MAN TWO	What do you think of the movie?
DJANET	What is this, ENTERTAINMENT TONIGHT?
MAN ONE	Thank heaven for liddle girls...
MAN TWO	Well, it beats 'Tarzan'.

Pause.

DJANET	Pardon me?
MAN TWO	Last week they showed Tarzan. 'Ivory in the Jungle'.
DJANET	You're kidding!
MAN TWO	I am quite serious.

DJANET   That's the one where the two hunters and the
          girl are trying to find some type of rare Ivory
          or something and the rare elephants that
          have these rare Ivory tusks roam freely in an
          area considered to be an ancient...

          Overlapping.

MAN TWO   ...Ancient, ancestral tribal burial ground. I
          am Benoit Viton Akonde. How do you do?

DJANET   You know, I don't think I've ever seen the end
          of GIGI.

MAN ONE   Thank heaven for little girls!

          *Djanet re-enters Ben's room. She reclines
          on the bed.*

          To Ben.

          Benoit Viton Akonde, 28, born in Benin,
          recently returned from France where you'd
          spent the past 10 years. I liked your style: A
          sort of Western/African. Fitted jeans under a
          traditional Dashiki. Cute, real cute and real...

          She sits up.

          When you took me to the palace. How in the
          hell did you get a key to the palace? And you
          say, quite nonchalantly, that your great
          grandfather was the last king of Abomey. So,
          you're my African prince, huh?

          At the palace, I get my own personal tour of
          the many buildings encircled in the ornately
          carved palace wall. All the black history I'd

ever learned in school suggested that black
history began with slavery. Well, I was now
standing in a place that suggested otherwise.

The throne room was amazing. Each king
had his own throne designed to his own
particular taste. And each had his own flag
which would symbolize what he wished for
his people. The rooms where filled with
ancient artifacts, carvings, utensils and
musical instruments, hundreds of years old.

She walks toward Ben. The sound of Da-
homian drums hover in the background.

I can still see the large building that was the
holding area for prisoners and slaves that
were to be sold off to the Europeans. I'd
never really made the connection that Africans had anything to do with the slave trade.
But it wasn't just that. I know that those Africans who did aid in the slave trade were
mainly protecting themselves. I knew that if
they didn't raid other nations and sell those
peoples to the Europeans, they themselves
would be at risk of becoming slaves. So it
wasn't just that.

Haitian drumming replace the Dahomian
drums, creating an ominous tension.

Remember that picture? The one that depicted the many ways in which the slaves
where piled up, one atop another in the slave
ships which were to cross the Atlantic Ocean
to the colonies.

I had seen pictures like this in history books.
But it wasn't just that.

Very slowly.

Swing low, sweet chariot.

400 years ago I, the descendant of slaves, may have stood
                  here myself.   And you, the descendant of Af-
                  rican kings, standing right behind me, would
                  have been selling me to the white man to save
                  your own life. This might actually be where
                  my journey began 400 years ago. And I could
                  see how we were packed like sardines. Fifteen
million human beings transported like canned fish, for
months on end, thousands of miles from home.

She sings.

Coming for to carry me home.

Then you put your hands on my shoulders. And we stood
                  there, glued to time for what seemed to be
                  hours.

                  Drumming ends.

                  Ben, I wasn't angry at you when we left the
                  palace that day, you know. Listen, I say these
                  words whenever I feel like I'm getting involved
                  in something dangerous. "Look, I'm really not
                  interested in seeing anyone on an intimate
                  basis right now. I relish my freedom and get
                  real demanding in relationships. I have a lot
                  of things to do with my life and I really don't
                  want to get tied down."

BEN   I see. So, what time should I pick you up
                  tomorrow then?

                  Slight pause.

DJANET   Ah... Ten's just fine with me.

            Shit!

            I was so embarrassed that day at the post
            office. I was just so excited to get a parcel
            from my family. I ripped the package open
            right then and there and several pairs of
            women's underwear in assorted pastel shades
            fell like autumn leaves to the ground — for
            everyone to see. And you just picked up my
            panties and stuffed them in your jacket
            pocket. Oh God!

            I didn't eat lunch that day. Too busy. Too
            busy crying over the packet of Dunhill ciga-
            rettes my sister Rosie sent me. Laughing at
            the CITY T.V. T-shirt my sister Terese sent
            me. The stuffed toy rabbit my baby sister
            Celia gave me, and the photos of all of them
            my parents sent me.

            What the hell am I doing here in my ancestral
            homeland, my cultural birthplace, feeling
            homesick.

            And I ask you why you came back to Benin.

BEN   Les Francais, ils sont racistes.

DJANET   Ben, you know you even have a way of mak-
            ing the word racist sound sexy.

BEN   In France I am a second class citizen. I get
            angry just thinking about it. After having
            spent most of my adult life in France, I felt
            that I now needed the comfort, is that the
            right word, the support of my own family and

my own culture.

DJANET   You knew what your culture was.

              Family, you said, is a strange phenomenon.
              No matter what happens, they...

                   Overlapping.

BEN   ...They are always your family. It is one of
              the strongest kinds of bonds we human
              beings ever know.

                   It is late at night. Djanet and Ben lay in bed.

BEN   Djanet?

DJANET   Yes Ben.

BEN   Are you sleeping?

DJANET   No sweetheart, I'm not sleeping.

BEN   Teach me that song again.

                   Singing.

DJANET   A.B.C.,

BEN   A.B.C.,

DJANET   Easy as 1, 2, 3.

BEN   Easy as 1, 2, 3.

DJANET   Simple as doh, rae, me,

BEN   Simple as doh, rae, me,

DJANET   A.B.C. 1,2,3, baby you and me.

BEN   A.B.C. 1,2,3, baby you and me.

DJANET & BEN   A.B.C.
                          Easy as 1, 2, 3,
                          Simple as doh, rae, me,
                          A.B.C. 1,2,3, baby you and me.

BEN   I like that song. Teach it to me again.

                          All traces of Ben dissolve .

                          The airport re-appears.

Airport   Air Afrique Flight 735 to Paris, London, New
Announcer   York and Buffalo, is now boarding. Will all
                          passengers kindly make their way to Gate
                          number 9.

DJANET   That's me. I'd better hurry.

                          Djanet pulls out a bottle of Grand Marnier.

                          It's not that I'm afraid of flying, it's just that I
                          like to be real relaxed when that thing takes
                          off. I prefer to have my two feet planted firmly
                          on the ground at all times. But since I have
                          no choice in the matter, I'd rather my brain
                          were flying too.

                          Here's to taking the train —

                          She drinks from the bottle.

                          — or walking!

                          She drinks again.

In the last year, I have walked so far, that if...

Let me tell you one more story. It's about... Well you'll see
        what it's about.

        At Epulu Station, in Zaire. I hire two rangers
        to guide me 28 kilometres into the Ituri rain
        forest — better known as the jungle to meet
        the BaMbuti people — better known as the
        Pygmies.

                *BaMbuti music begins. A sound collage of
                voice and Mbira (Central African thump
                piano).*

        Now, the jungle out of this world, because of
        the thick canopy of trees and flora, it's always
        either twilight or pitch black. And it stinks in
        the jungle. Seriously, everything is either
        dying, dead or coming back to life. And
        when you walk in the jungle, you sink about
        10 centimetres down into the ground with
        each step, into   layer after layer of this dying,
        dead or coming back to life stuff.

        We walk for nine hours to get to this particu-
        lar BaMbuti settlement. Nine full hours. But
        when we finally arrive at the encampment the
        chief comes out to greet us.

        Now, I've never stood face to face with a real
        live Pygmy before and the first thing that you
        notice about him is that he's really — short.

        The clan must have had a good days hunting
        because he immediately invites us in to eat
        with them. The choice of entree: Roast
        Monkey or — Dik-dik.

        Now, I would have selected the Monkey

because I pride myself on being able to question cultural taboos. But when we entered
the encampment, there they were, still skin-
ning it. So, I chose the — Dik-dik.

The Dik-dik was great, real juicy and tender -
Dik-dik, by the way, is a very small antelope
that inhabits that particular part of the
jungle.

After supper, we joined the BaMbutis around
the fire. One of the men around the small
bonfire slowly brought out some leaves. He
placed them on a small metal disk and began
to cook them over the fire. Mmn, I figured,
dessert! Then he crushed the leaves up with
his fingers and placed them into the bowl of a
very, very long pipe. He lit the tobacco and
inhaled slowly.

A familiar scent hovered above us in the dark
jungle night air.

He then proceeded to pass the pipe around. I
— well, once the pipe came to me, I —

She inhales the smoke and chokes.

Jesus! The Rastafarians have nothing on the
pygmies!

While the pipe is doing the rounds, I notice
that across the burning fire from me, one of
the BaMbuti men is doing something real
peculiar to the two small branches he's
holding. He keeps splitting the branches to a
point half way down it's length, until each of
the branches begins to resemble a kind of
rough hand broom. Then he starts knocking

one branch against the other and it makes a
kind of rattling percussive sound. His
rhythm is slow but precise. Then he begins
to sing and in no time the rest of the clan
joins him.

The BaMbuti chant is heard

And oh, the melodies and harmonies they
created were just so — I'd never heard anything like it. Underscored by the rattling
percussive rhythm they were building this
pyramid, in song.

Suddenly had a brain-storm. I knew a song
that came from the jungle — I had heard it so
many times in the Tarzan movies. So, I just
start singing:

> Won di
> Won di eh my heh oh.

> Won di
> Won di eh my heh oh.

> Won di
> Won di eh my heh oh.

Well they don't get it. So I figure, like , maybe
I'm in the wrong key. In the Tarzan movies
they always sang it really high, and I just
figured that it was because they were actually
southern black baptists in drag:

> Won di
> Won di eh my heh oh.

Won di
Won di eh my heh oh.

Won di...

They just didn't recognize it at all, much less
like it.

Listening to BaMbuti music is like a lesson in
the true forms of jazz improvisation and
harmonies. Every one has their own part and
knows exactly where they fit in.

Meanwhile, recovering from my first attempt
at cross cultural communication, I remember
another song, this one an actual BaMbuti
chant that I learned in school. I figured
they'd be really choked to hear this coming
from my mouth:

>   Dja dja dja dja,
>   Mchok mdja.
>   Dja,
>   Mchok mdja.
>
>   Dja dja dja dja,
>   Mchok mdja.
>   Dja,
>   Mchok Mdja.

Well... they didn't know this one either — but
they loved it. At first they sang the words
wrong, but they soon hooked into the rhythm
of the chant.

Man One and Two join her.

ALL   Dja dja dja dja,

Mchok mdja.
Dja,
Mchok mdja.

Dja dja dja dja,
Mchok mdja.
Dja,
Mchok Mdja.

And we didn't stop singing that song for
about twenty minutes.

BaMbuti music is — heavenly, yes, that's the
word, just plain heavenly.

While they were singing, I began to think,
that well, I should at least sing them a song
from Canada, a song that rang with the true
essence of Canadiana. But I couldn't think of
one. It was like every Canadian song that I
had ever learned leapt out of my brain and
choose that particular moment to do it. A
Canadian song... Canadian song... Canadian
song...

Singing.

Oh Canada, our home and native
land.
True patriot love, in all thy sons
command.
With...

Now, I don't know whether it was a side effect
of the particular brand of tobacco that we'd
been smoking, but I was getting this sixth
sense that they weren't really, well, really
liking it. So trusting my instincts and
subordinating reason:

*She sings the anthem like an intense soulful
gospel ballad.*

> With glowing hearts,
> We see thee rise,
> The true north strong and free.
> From far and wide,
> Oh oh oh Canadaah,
> We stand on guard for thee-e-e-e.
> Ohhh Canadaaaaaaaah,
> Gloooorious and freeee-e-eee-e.
> We stand on guard, we stand on guard
> for theeeeeee.
> Oooohhhh Caaa-naa-daaaahhh,
> We stand on Guaaaaard for-or or
> theee-ee-e-he-e-e-e-heee.

Well, they just loved it!

That night, I slept in the encampment. They
offered us their huts for the night, they are so
kind. So we offered them our tents. And as I
lay in my sleeping bag on the straw mat, I
began to think: Here I am in a BaMbuti hut,
in the middle of the Ituri rain forest, in Zaire,
in Africa, on the planet earth, the third planet
from the sun in the milky way, situated in an
unknown quadrant of the universe - in what?
What comes after universe? What's the
universe in? And why was being here so
special? And — I couldn't figure it out,
except that, it had something to do with —

*She sings a phrase of the anthem slowly,
again in a soulful gospel style.*

From far and wide...

That's it! See, that's me! The African heart-
beat in a Canadian song.

African Canadian. Not coloured, or negro...
Maybe not even black. African Canadian.

And I closed my eyes, and even though I had
to have my legs protruding from the doorway
of the hut, because their huts are so small, I
began to feel right at home.

The airport re-appears.

Airport   Mr. Benoit Akonde paging Miss Janet Sears.
Announcer   Would Miss Janet Sears please pick up the
                        courtesy telephone at the Air Afrique ticket
                        counter.

> *The courtesy telephone rings. Djanet slowly
> moves toward it, pauses for a moment and
> then picks up the receiver.*

Hi Ben...

Mon chere, c'est n'est pas a faut de toi. C'est
parce'que... Look, I'm going to have to speak
to you in English, mon petit... O.k., is this
slow enough for you... But, I tried to explain
everything in the letter...

Pause.

Ben, I cannot just be your wife. I must have
something of my own, too. Maybe I need to
tell people about what I've seen here. There
are lots of people back home who need to
hear about this place, who need to hear how
important they are. Maybe that's it... I am an
African, Ben, an African of the Americas. I

belong to the African diaspora.   Africa will always be here for me... I know, I know you might not be...

Pause.

Come with me, Ben. I'm serious, come with me... Shit, we'll move to Quebec...

Pause.

Silly, of course I'll write you... I said, do not be so silly, of course I will write to you... I don't think customs allows mangoes through the post, sweetheart... I didn't forget it, I left the T-shirt there for you. And every time someone asks you what CITY T.V. means —

Airport Announcer   This is a final boarding call for all passengers on Air Afrique flight 735, on route to Paris, London and Buffalo. Would all passengers on Air Afrique flight 735 please proceed to gate number 9.

She looks in the direction of the gate, and then back again at the telephone in her hand.

DJANET   Ben —

She hesitates.

They're calling my flight... I... O.k? Yeh, you take care of yourself too. Yeh... I love you too, Benoit Viton Akonde. I love you too.

She pauses for a moment, then replaces the receiver.

I was going home — to Canada.   Yeh.   I had
all my history on my back.   The base of my
whole culture would be forever with me.   And
funny thing is, it always had been.   In my
thighs, my behind, my hair, my lips.

She goes to pick up her hand luggage .

Did you know that the Sphinx' nose had
originally been Negroid — No.   Did you know
that the Sphinx' nose had originally been
African and that when the first European
scientific mission found it in the nineteenth
century, they chopped the Sphinx' nose off.

Michael Jackson chopped his nose off too. It's
true!

Singing.

> Young, gifted and black
> Oh what a lovely, precious dream.
>
> There were times when I felt so
> insecure
> Never sure
> Where I fit in.
> So I tried to be more like someone else
> But it left me feeling empty inside
>
> No matter what people say to me,
> I've got to find my own way to be
> My own way to be:
>
> Inside my African Heart
> Beats a special part
> That gives me strength, gives me life
> Inside my African Soul

Is where I found the light
That makes me feel right, makes me
whole.

Now I know where to look to find
myself.
I need someone to share their love
with me
But I've got to find my own way to be
My own way to be:

Inside my African Heart
Beats a special part
That gives me strength, gives me life
Inside my African Soul
Is where I found the light
That makes me feel right, makes me
whole.

Inside, Inside...

> *A powerful west African Rhythm*
> *emerges.*

In - a - side, In - a - side,
In - a - side,
In - a - side in my soul,

In - a - side, In - a - side,
In - a - side,
In - a - side in my soul.

Inside, Inside...

Djanet turns in the direction of the depar-
ture gate, but catches her own reflection

*In an imaginery glass door, in the waiting
area. She stares at herself. She adjusts her
T-shirt and wrap, then reaches into the
cloth bag and pulls out a brilliantly embroidered west African Boubou. She realizes
that if she doesn't hurry she'll miss her flight,
but takes the time to make the Boubou
look just right.*

*The cloth bag is now empty. Djanet un-
knots it revealing the original length of west
African fabric. She wraps the fabric around
her head.*

*She stares intensely at her reflection. She
smiles.*

You know sometimes when you look into the
mirror and you sorta' — catch your own I
(sic).

*She sings the 'Carmen Jones' song in her
own Canadian/Caribbean/British style over
the intense African rhythm.*

That's love
That's love
That's love
That's love

*The music stops abruptly. Her metamor-
phasis is now complete.*

Dorothy Dandridge, eat your heart out, I am
beautiful.

BLACKOUT

*In the blackout, Man One and Man Two
begin an Sunnu rhythm on the cow bell,
Djundjun and Djembe. As the lights come
up for the curtain call, Djanet, Man One
and Man Two sing, releasing the incanta-
tion and ending the play.*

Ay yeh denumba,
Acoe,
Bena bee sema roe,
Dumumba.

Ay yeh denumba,
Acoe,
Bena bee sema roe,
Dumumba.

Repeat.

CURTAIN.

AFTERWORD

> '*The longing to tell one's story and the process of telling is symbolically a gesture of longing to recover the past in such a way that one experiences both a sense of reunion and a sense of release.'*
>
> Bell Hooks

AFRIKA SOLO falls into a category of writing that Audre Lorde calls autobio-mythography. The play is both fictional and autobiographical, loosely based upon a year long journey that I took across the breadth and some of the length of Africa. A journey that changed my perceptions of the world; a journey that changed my perception of me in the world.

I was born in England and raised both in England and Canada, where I presently live. My mother is from Jamaica and my father from Guyana, two different countries in the Caribbean. I had, until very recently, read little, to no literature that reflected my life, that stated my concerns, that told my stories. I grew up in a society where I was considered a minority, minor, inferior, and somewhere along the line, I developed a type of internalized oppression. Although the ways in which each of us experiences internalized oppression are unique, no black person in this society has been spared.' 'Internalized racism' has been the primary means by which we have been forced to perpetuate and "agree" to our own oppression.

My education, for the most part, taught me a history that suggested that African people were primitive savages or were placed here on earth to serve, due to our inferior intelligence and natures. My parents can fill an encyclopedia with stories of their emigration to Britain in the 50s. People actually walked behind them to see if they in fact had tails.

I was born in Britain, but did not belong. Where in fact did I belong? I am a naturalized citizen of Canada. What do I

answer when people constantly ask me, where I'm from?
The Caribbean, even though I've never lived there? And
which of my parents' countries would I choose? There is
one common denominator, though, Africa. But how could I
claim a continent and cultures that I knew virtually nothing
about?

I could not foresee the mammoth effect a journey to Africa
would make on my life. 'The African continent is larger and
more diverse than most of us have realized. Its climates
range from arid to tropical, its topography from desert to
grassland to dense rain forest to snow -covered mountains.
Its people live in fifty-four nations and speak over two thousand languages and dialects. In parts of Ethiopia or Bu-
rundi, the people are likely to be over six feet in height,
while in areas of central Africa or Namibia, any one reaching
five feet would be considered tall.'

I encourage all peoples of African descent to make a con-
certed effort to visit Africa. And here, I am not advocating
relocation. An African leader, while addressing a gathering
of African Americans in Los Angeles, during African Heritage
Month, welcomed us back with open arms, if we indeed
wished to return to the continent of our ancestry. But went
on to state, that since we had been here for 400 years, we
had, in fact, built this land and therefore had every right to
fight for it.

The reality though, is that not all of us will get an opportu-
nity to make this journey. That is why I felt a need to share
my experience. I wrote this play because there are still
many like me, who have and are still suffering as a direct
result of living or more so from being born and growing up
in a systemically racist society. This is also their story.

Stylistically, AFRIKA SOLO, follows a traditional West
African genre that I call, "Sundiata Form". Traditional West
African theatre consists of a story being told through narra-
tive, music and dance. (Finances alone have prevented me
from producing the play with an ensemble of dancers.)
"Sundiata Form" is inclusive and involves using all the per-

formance mediums. We here in the diaspora have only
begun to experiment with the fullness of this form.

Musically, the score and songs, co-composed by Allen
Booth, Rudi Quammie Williams and myself, are veritably
microcosm of African music, that is, everything from traditional African music, as in BaMbuti music, to contemporary
African music from Africa and the diaspora, as in `High Life',
Rap and R & B. The score is organic in nature, in that it
conceptually reflected the major themes and ethnographic
concerns of the play.

I had fully intended this afterword to contain a short chronology of African history, from pre-colonial times to the
present and to include important diasporic references. In
the midst of collecting the data I realized the mammoth
nature of this task. Even a short chronology would encom-
pass several volumes. I did, however, want to chronicle
some of the information that influenced me and cite my references in a bibliography, I felt that those interested in
further investigation, would be given some hints as to where
to go in order to whet their appetites.

The following is a list of a few interesting facts about African
history that you may not be aware of:

- Aesop, the reknown fabilist, was a black samian slave.
  He lived during the sixth century B.C. and was born to
  Ethopian parents.

- Egypt, located in Northwest Africa was, contrary to
  popular belief, an Arican civilization.

- The Egyptian Sphinx of Gizeh, the oldest statue in the
  world, bears the face of a Black person.

- Europe's earliest historian, Herodotus, and evidence describes Egypt to be the cradle of European civilization.

- Matthew Henson, a Black man from New York was in fact the first known human being to reach the North Pole. He arrived arrived April 6th, 1909.

- Dr. Daniel Williams, a Black Chicago surgeon was the first to perfom a successful operation on the human heart.

- Black Madonnas ("Virgin Marys") around the world (especially in Europe) are left from the pre-christian worship of the Black Egyptian Goddess, Isis.

a) Christianity incorporated some of the Isis legend after unsuccessful attempts to outlaw the cult.

b) These sacred statues and painting are still credited with numerous miracles.

- Hannibal, a Black African from Carthage, performed the astounding feat of crossing the Alps in 210 B.C., where he defeated Rome in every battle for fifteen years.

a) Hannibal invaded and occupied Italy for twelve years with 26,000 warriors (to Rome's 1,000,000 warriors).

b) Coins depicting Hannibal from his time, show him as African.

c) Hannibal's military strategies are still studied in military academies.

- Alexander Sergeyvich Pushkin (1799-1837), one of the greatest names in Russian literature, was the great-grandson of Hannibal.

- "The Real McCoy":, a testimony of genuine dependabil-
  ity, refers to the work of Black inventor Elijah Mccoy
  and his highly esteemed lubricating systems.

- Traditional world maps (Mercator maps) are grossly dis-
  torted, exaggerating the sizes of White (European and
  North American) nations.

a) Mercator shows Europe larger than South America
   which in truth is nearly double the size of Europe.

b) Mercator shows the Soviet Union to be more than
   double the size of Africa, though Africa is much larger.

The United Nations has recently published a "New" World
Map with true proportions.

- Delphos, founder of the Delphic Oracle of ancient
  Greece, was Black, as depicted on coins from that
  period.

- Mansa Musa ruled the Kingdom of Mali, (a nation
  founded in Paleolithic times), at the height of its
  existence, in 1307 -1324. He is responsible for building one of the first universites on this planet, in Tombouctou, in 1324.

- Sonni Ali Ber, defeated Mansa Musa, capturing the Kindom of Mali and founded of the Kingdom of Songhai.
  His empire included such flourishing cities as Djenne
  and Tombouctou, and at the height of its power
  stretched from the Atlantic to Anglo Egyptian Sudan.

- Imhotep, of ancient Egypt, was the true father of Medicine. He lived in 2,780 B.C., and diagnosed and
  treated over 200 different diseases.

a) Hippocates' Creed (doctors' oath) pays tribute to Imhotep in the first sentence.

b) Imhotep was also a priest, scribe, astronomer and was
the architect responsible for the building of the
"stepped Pyramid".

- The Ganges, the sacred river of India, is named after an
Ethopian king who conquered Asia as far as this river.

- In 1310 A.D., Abubakari II, leading 2,000 ships, sailed
out of the Senegal River in the Kingdom of Mali, to the
Atlantic and onto the 'New World', 180 years before
Columbus. He is an Ancestor of Kunta Kinte, enslaved
400 years later.

- The Kingdom of Kumbi (or Ghana), existed in 300 A.D.
(although the 1st known record, is autually 1,000
years older.

- In 266 A.D., Queen Zenobia, became the Queen of
Palmyra. She is credited with conquering Egypt,
much to the dismay of Rome.

- In 1582, Nzinga, Warrior Queen of the Matamba nation,
in Angola, trained an army of women and men and
waged war against the Portuguese, who were seizing
her country. After 15 bloody years she surrendered
and only because her spears and bows and arrows
were no match for their cannons and guns.

- In 120 B.C., Publus Terentius Afer (for African), or Ter-
ence, the playwright, became one of Rome's greatest
stylists and writer of comedies. Author of over 400
pieces, some of his immortal comedies are: Andria;
The Mother-in-law; The Self Avenger and The Eun-
nuch.

- In 1580 B.C., The Land of Punt, was the third kingdom

of the Nile. Presently where Ethiopia and Somalia lie, home of the Abyssinians.

Many of these facts have been omitted from the history books used in the conventional 'western' education system. Please refer to the bibliography if you would like to investigate this further.

Renowned African historian, Professor Ali Mazrui, points out, 'people will not look forward to posterity who never looked back to their ancestors'. Finding out about my history and learning about the stories of my ancestors was like finding myself standing on a path that extended far behind me, a path that also allowed me to see several, once invisible, roads that lay ahead. While in Africa, I was in the majority for one of the first times in my life. The colour of my skin was not an issue and the content of my character shone. For the first time in my life, I felt I had a right to take up space on this planet, and it felt good.

Djanet Sears

Bibliography

The following references may be used as jumping off points for further investigation, since these books contain fairly concise bibliographies themselves.

BEN-JOCHANNAN, Yosef A. *Black Man of The Nile and His Family.* Alkebu-lan Books Assoc.: New York, 1972.

DAVIDSON, Basil. *The History of West Africa.* Longman Press: London, 1977.

DIOP, Cheikh Anta. *The African Origin of Civilization, Myth or Reality.* Lawrence Hill & Co.: Westport, 1967.

DU BOIS, W.E.B. *The World and Africa.* International Publishers: New York, 1965.

HOOKS, Bell. *Talking Back.* Southend Press: Boston, 1988.

HOOKS, Bell. *From Margin to Center.* Southend Press: Boston, 1984.

HOOKS, Bell. *Ain't I A Woman.* Southend Press: Boston, 1981.

HULTMAN, Tami. *The Africa News Cookbook.* Viking Penguin Inc: New York, 1987.

HYMAN, Mark. *Blacks Before America.* (Radio Transcripts Compiled). Bell Of Pennsylvania: Philadelphia, 1976?

LIPSKY, Suzanne. *Re-evaluation Councelling.* Black Re-emergence: Internalized Oppression. New York: (Pamphlet).

PUSHKIN, Alexander. *The Queen of Spades and Other Stories.* Penguin Books Ltd: Middlesex, 1979.

ROGERS, J. A. *100 Amazing Facts About The Negro.* Helga M. Rogers Press: New York, 1957.

ROGERS, J. A. *Sex And Race, Vols. I, II & III.* Helga M. Rogers Press: New York, 1940.

ROGERS, J. A. *World's Great Men of Colour.* Collier Books: New York, 1946.

X, Malcolm. *Malcolm X on Afro-American History.* Pathfinder: New York, 1988.

REVIEWS

Clever, insightful and devilishliy humourous.

Vit Wagner
The Toronto Star

Afrika Solo is one witty and perceptive woman's funny and touching account of her own very special voyage of self discovery, a voyage an audience can share and savor.

Barbara Cooke
The Ottawa Citizen